SIMPLE MACHINES

A Sesame Street Science Book

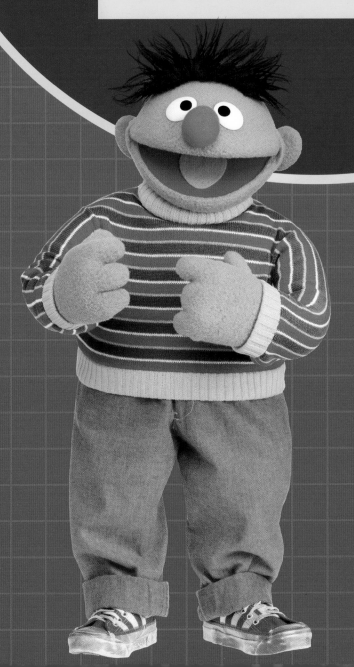

Marie-Therese Miller

Lerner Publications ◆ Minneapolis

Sesame Street has always been a community of curiosity and exploration. We know that all children are naturally curious about the world around them. Understanding basic science concepts can be fun for everyone in the neighborhood—including kids! In the Sesame Street® World of Science books, *Sesame Street*'s favorite furry friends help young readers learn about how the world works.

Sincerely,

The Editors at Sesame Workshop

Table of Contents

SIMPLE MACHINES ARE EVERYWHERE

Simple machines are tools that help make some things easier to do.

Simple machines help me lift my boxes of birdseed.

THE SIX SIMPLE MACHINES

These are the six simple machines:

1. inclined plane

2. lever

3. wheel and axle

4. pulley

5. wedge

6. screw

Simple machines help people do lots of different things.

An inclined plane is a flat surface that is raised at one end. Inclined planes help with moving and lifting from high to low or low to high.

Wheelchair ramps are inclined planes. My Papi uses a wheelchair ramp instead of stairs.

A lever is a stiff board or bar
that helps move or lift objects.

I use a shovel to dig dirt in my fairy garden. A shovel is a lever.

Paddles, seesaws, and light switches are levers.

Another simple machine is the wheel and axle. A wheel is shaped like a circle. An axle is a rod that connects to the center of a wheel.

The wheel and axle spin together.

Roller skates and scooters have wheels and axles that move them. A Ferris wheel has a wheel and axle too.

A rolling pin is a wheel and axle. It helps me flatten yummy cookie dough.

A pulley is a wheel with a rope looped over it. An object attaches to one end of the rope. A person pulls the other end of the rope to lift the object.

We use a pulley to raise the flag at school.

Wedges are tools that are thicker at one end and thinner at the other end. Sometimes they are used to split things apart.

Did you know that knives are wedges?

Wedges can also keep something in place. A doorstop is a wedge. It keeps the door in place.

My dance teacher uses a wedge to keep the classroom door open.

23

Another simple machine is a screw. A screw is a cylinder with a spiral groove around it. Screws keep things together.

Simple machines help make it easier to do all kinds of work. You can see simple machines everywhere.

Science All Around

Can you guess these simple machines? Check your answers on page 30.

What kind of simple machine helps a skateboard roll?

A playground slide moves people from high to low.

What type of simple machine is a slide?

Glossary

axle: a rod that connects to the center of a wheel that helps the wheel turn

pulley: a wheel with a rope looped over it that is used to move things

ramp: a flat surface that connects something high with something low

wedge: a tool that is thick on one end and thin on the other; can be used to split something apart or keep something in place

Answers to Science All Around

A wheel and axle help a skateboard roll.
A slide is an inclined plane.

Learn More

Barger, Jeff. *Wheel and Axle*. Vero Beach, FL: Rourke Educational Media, 2019.

Katz, Susan B. *Push and Pull: A Sesame Street Science Book*. Minneapolis: Lerner Publications, 2023.

Wesley, Maggie S. *Wheels and Axles at Work*. New York: Enslow, 2022.

Index

Photo Acknowledgments

Image credits: Ariel Skelley/Getty Images, p. 5; gpetric/Getty Images, pp. 6 (1), 26 (top left); Thana Prasongsin/Getty Images, pp. 6 (2), 26 (top right); Image Source/Getty Images, pp. 6 (3), 26 (middle left); DougSchneiderPhoto/Getty Images, pp. 7 (4), 26 (middle right); necati bahadir bermek/Getty Images, pp. 7 (5), 26 (bottom left); Enrique Ramos López/Getty Images, pp. 7 (6), 26 (bottom right); Brian Mitchell/Getty Images, p. 8; yamasan/Getty Images, p. 10; sianc/Getty Images, p. 12 (top); Tang Ming Tung/Getty Images, p. 12 (bottom left); cunaplus/Shutterstock, p. 12 (bottom right); Rafael Ben-Ari/Getty Images, p. 14; ViewStock/Getty Images, p. 16 (left); holgs/Getty Images, p. 16 (right); Prostock-Studio/Getty Images, p. 17; José Antonio Luque Olmedo/Getty Images, p. 18; Caspar Benson/Getty Images, p. 19; RapidEye/Getty Images, p. 21; jpgfactory/Getty Images, p. 22; robcruse/Getty Images, p. 23; SolStock/Getty Images, p. 24 (bottom); jennygiraffe/Shutterstock, p. 24 (circle); Sollina Images/Getty Images, p. 28; JohnnyGreig/Getty Images, p. 29.

Cover: PeopleImages/Getty Images.

With appreciation to all scientists and engineers, particularly John, Michelle, Meghan, John Vincent, Erin, Elizabeth, and future scientist Greyson

Lerner Publications Company
An imprint of Lerner Publishing Group, Inc.
241 First Avenue North
Minneapolis, MN 55401 USA

For reading levels and more information, look up this title at www.lernerbooks.com.

Main body text set in Mikado.
Typeface provided by HVD.

Editor: Amber Ross **Designer:** Mary Ross
Photo Editor: Annie Zheng

Library of Congress Cataloging-in-Publication Data

Names: Miller, Marie-Therese, author.
Title: Simple machines: A Sesame Street ® science book / Marie-Therese Miller.
Description: Minneapolis : Lerner Publications , [2023] | Series: Sesame Street ® World of Science | Includes bibliographical references and index. | Audience: Ages 4–8 | Audience: Grades K–1 | Summary: "Simple machines are tools that make work easier to do. Sesame Street characters help make learning about the six simple machines accessible and engaging for young learners"– Provided by publisher.
Identifiers: LCCN 2022015522 (print) | LCCN 2022015523 (ebook) | ISBN 9781728475790 (library binding) | ISBN 9781728486161 (paperback) | ISBN 9781728484785 (ebook)
Subjects: LCSH: Simple machines—Juvenile literature.
Classification: LCC TJ147 .M537 2023 (print) | LCC TJ147 (ebook) | DDC 621.8—dc23/eng20220708

LC record available at https://lccn.loc.gov/2022015522
LC ebook record available at https://lccn.loc.gov/2022015523

Manufactured in the United States of America
1-52146-50609-7/1/2022